Let's Celebrate

EMANCIPATION DAY & JUNETEENTH

BY Barbara deRubertis

Kane Press
New York

For activities and resources for this book and others in the HOLIDAYS & HEROES series, visit: www.kanepress.com/holidays-and-heroes

Text copyright © 2018 by Barbara deRubertis
Photographs/images copyrights: Cover: © Jacob 09/Shutterstock; page 1: © Monkey Business Images/Shutterstock; page 3: © Billy Calzada/Zumapress/Newscom; page 4: © Everett Historical/Shutterstock; page 5: © Everett Historical/Shutterstock; page 6 top: © National Archives/NARA; page 6 bottom: © Razoom Game/Shutterstock; page 7: © The Miriam and Ira D. Wallach Division of Art, Prints and Photographs: Photography Collection, The New York Public Library; page 8 top: © Library of Congress, Prints and Photographs Division, LC-USZ62-40758; page 8 inset 1: © Neftali/Shutterstock; page 8 inset 2: © Rook 76/Shutterstock; page 8 inset 3: © Neftali/Shutterstock; page 9: © Everett Historical/Shutterstock; page 10: © Library of Congress, Prints and Photographs Division, LC-DIG-pga-03004; page 10 inset: © Everett Collection Inc/Alamy Stock Photo; page 11: © Library of Congress, Prints and Photographs Division, LC-USZ62-93268; page 12: © Architect of the Capitol/ Artis Lane, sculptor; page 13: © Library of Congress, Prints and Photographs Division, LC-DIG-ppmsca-52069; page 14: © Library of Congress, Prints and Photographs Division, LC-DIG-ppmsca-54230; page 15: © Everett Historical/Shutterstock; page 16: © Library of Congress, Prints and Photographs Division, LC-DIG-pga-03235; page 16 inset: © Rainer Lesniewski/ Shutterstock; page 17: © Library of Congress, Prints and Photographs Division, LC-DIG-ppmsca-19241; page 18: © Library of Congress, Prints and Photographs Division, LC-DIG-ppmsca-18444; page 19: © Library of Congress, Prints and Photographs Division, LC-DIG-ds-0; page 20: © MPVHistory/Alamy Stock Photo; page 21: © Library of Congress, Prints and Photographs Division, LC-DIG-ppmsca-34584; page 22: © Harper's/Library of Congress, LOC-LC-USZ62-127599; page 23 top: © Everett Historical/Shutterstock; page 23 inset: © Library of Congress, Prints and Photographs Division, LC-DIG-ds-03296; page 24: © Tom Williams/Roll Call Photos/Newscom; page 25: © Library of Congress, Prints and Photographs Division, LC-DIG-pga-02797; page 26: © Library of Congress, Prints and Photographs Division, LC-DIG-pga-08518; page 26 inset: © Library of Congress, Prints and Photographs Division, LC-DIG-cwpb-05697; page 27: © Calyx22 | Dreamstime.com; page 28: © Steve Gonzales/Houston Chronicle/Associated Press; page 29: © Viktoria Hodos/Shutterstock; page 30: © Melissa Lyttle/Zuma Press/ Newscom; page 31: ©Ricky Fitchett/Zuma Press/Newscom; page 32: © Jacob 09/Shutterstock; back cover: © Monkey Business Images/Shutterstock
All due diligence has been conducted in identifying copyright holders and obtaining permissions.

Library of Congress Cataloging-in-Publication Data

Names: deRubertis, Barbara, author.
Title: Let's celebrate Emancipation Day & Juneteenth / by Barbara deRubertis.
Description: New York : Kane Press, 2018. | Series: Holidays & heroes
Identifiers: LCCN 2017051917 (print) | LCCN 2017052195 (ebook) | ISBN
  9781635920628 (ebook) | ISBN 9781635920604 (reinforced library binding : alk.
  paper) | ISBN 9781635920611 (pbk. : alk. paper)
Subjects: LCSH: Juneteenth--Juvenile literature. |
  Slaves--Emancipation--Texas--Anniversaries, etc.--Juvenile literature. |
  Slaves--Emancipation--United States--Anniversaries, etc.--Juvenile
  literature. | African Americans--Anniversaries, etc.--Juvenile literature.
Classification: LCC E185.93.T4 (ebook) | LCC E185.93.T4 D47 2018 (print) |
  DDC 326/.809764--dc23
LC record available at https://lccn.loc.gov/2017051917

10 9 8 7 6 5 4 3 2 1

First published in the United States of America in 2018 by Kane Press, Inc.
Printed in China

Book Design and Photograph/Image Research: Maura Taboubi

Visit us online at **www.kanepress.com.**

Like us on Facebook
facebook.com/kanepress

Follow us on Twitter
@KanePress

Americans history is filled with stories of people working for noble causes—like freedom, justice, and equality.

But there was also a *terrible* part of America's history called *slavery*. This allowed people to own other people—as if they were property.

It took about 250 years, a war, and three kinds of legal action to finally end slavery.

The freeing of enslaved people is called "Emancipation." It is celebrated on two different dates in our country. The District of Columbia celebrates on April 16th. Texas and 45 other states celebrate on June 19th—or "Juneteenth."

Young girls celebrate Juneteenth in Texas.

Africans are brought to America to be sold as slaves.

How Did Slavery Begin in America?

Traders brought the first African slaves to the American colonies in 1619. As time passed, more and more free black Africans were captured and shipped across the ocean in chains. Those who survived were sold in slave markets.

If enslaved people later had children, they were slaves too. These children were often taken away from their parents and sold.

White plantation owners in the South bought the largest numbers of slaves. The huge cotton fields there required a lot of hard work. The owners came to depend on slaves to get the work done.

Enslaved Africans are sold at auction.

On July 4, 1776, the Declaration of Independence was signed. It said that the American colonies had formed a new country—the United States of America.

The Declaration also said that "all men are created equal." But this "equality" certainly did

not include slaves! And what about everyone having the rights to "life, liberty, and the pursuit of happiness"? Well, that didn't include slaves, either.

A slave in shackles

Child slaves in a cotton field

Many people thought slavery should be *abolished*—or ended. By 1804, all the northern states had either ended slavery or were beginning to end it gradually. For example, all children born in Pennsylvania after 1780 were free, even if their parents were enslaved.

But the states in the South would not give up their slaves.

Frederick Douglass stamp

Above: Declaration of the
Anti-Slavery Convention, 1833

Sojourner Truth stamp

Harriet Tubman stamp

During the 1800s, many *abolitionists* worked together to end slavery. The abolitionists were black and white, women and men.

Three of the most famous were Frederick Douglass, Sojourner Truth, and Harriet Tubman.

Frederick Douglass

Born into slavery, Frederick Douglass learned to read as a child. This would be a key to his future success.

Teaching a slave to read was illegal. But this didn't stop Douglass. He began teaching other slaves to read. The plantation owners found out . . . and were furious. They put an end to that!

Douglass escaped from slavery at age 20. Soon he joined the abolitionists in their work.

Frederick Douglass

Douglass was a gifted speaker and writer. He gave powerful speeches at anti-slavery meetings. He published an important anti-slavery newspaper. And his three books about his own life became bestsellers.

Over and over again, Douglass would ask, "What is the very *worst* thing slave owners do to their slaves?" People expected him to answer that it was the horrid, brutal treatment the slaves often suffered. But

African Americans shake hands with Douglass in his office in city hall, 1877.

Douglass would answer, *"Slave owners won't allow their slaves to be educated!"*

The most famous speech Douglass gave was "What, to the American Slave, Is the 4th of July?" He pointed out that enslaved people were not enjoying the rights listed in the Declaration of Independence.

Slaves were NOT being treated as equals. And they were NOT enjoying life, liberty, and the pursuit of happiness. Douglass said, "This Fourth of July is *yours*, not *mine*."

Frederick Douglass was an example of the greatness that former slaves could achieve—if they were educated and free.

Left: A print from 1883 honors the achievements of several former slaves, including Frederick Douglass.
Inset: Frederick Douglass published and wrote for the anti-slavery newspaper *The North Star*.

Sojourner Truth

Sojourner Truth was born into slavery in New York. But she was freed as a young woman. She spent most of her life fighting for women's rights and for an end to slavery.

Truth was a powerful woman. At six feet tall, she immediately got people's attention. But it was her speeches and her way of expressing ideas that made people listen.

Truth also had a deep, beautiful singing voice. When she gave a speech, she often sang songs she had written. In this way, she reached people's hearts as well as their minds.

She once said, "I tell you I can't read a book, but I can read . . . people."

A bust of Sojourner Truth in the U.S. Capitol

Sojourner Truth

Harriet Tubman

Harriet Tubman

Harriet Tubman was more famous for her abolitionist *actions* than for her words.

Tubman was only five feet tall, but she was fierce!

Tubman escaped from slavery in 1849, when she was 29 years old. She then worked for ten years as a "conductor" for the "Underground Railroad."

This railroad was not really underground, and it had no tracks or trains. It was a secret network of people who helped runaway slaves reach freedom.

Tubman made 19 trips into southern slave states. She led 300 slaves to northern free states or to Canada. Their dangerous journeys were made mostly in the dark of night, following the North Star.

And Harriet Tubman never lost a single "passenger" on her railroad.

People escape slavery on the Underground Railroad, 1863

The Civil War

The argument about slavery grew into a war between the northern and southern states—the Civil War.

The northern states opposed slavery. They were still the United States of America.

The southern states wanted to keep slavery. They formed a *new* country—the Confederate States of America.

Abraham Lincoln was President of the United States during this difficult time. Early in the war, Lincoln worked with Congress to pass a Compensated Emancipation Act.

Abraham Lincoln

Compensated emancipation meant that slave owners would be *paid* for each freed slave.

This act would apply only to slaves in the District of Columbia and in four "border states" (on the border between the North and the South).

Lincoln believed this peaceful solution to slavery could end the war. But none of the border states accepted his offer.

Left: A Civil War battle
Map: The United States when the war began in 1861
    Green: Union states without slavery
    Yellow: Union states with slavery
    Red: Confederate states
    Purple: Territories

President Lincoln hard at work on the Emancipation Proclamation

So Congress passed an act that provided for compensated emancipation only in the District of Columbia. This is the location of the nation's capital, Washington, D.C. It is not part of any state.

On **April 16, 1862,** President Lincoln signed the **District of Columbia Compensated Emancipation Act** into law.

Across America, some slave owners had already freed their slaves. Some had let their slaves earn wages and buy their freedom. Others had written wills that gave their slaves freedom when the owners died. Also, some state governments had freed the slaves in their states.

But the 3,000 enslaved people in the District of Columbia were the first to be freed by the *United States* government.

A large crowd of African Americans celebrates the end of slavery in Washington, D.C.

On **January 1, 1863,** President
Lincoln signed an executive order called
the **Emancipation Proclamation**. It freed
all the slaves in the Confederate States.

But the proclamation could only be
enforced in those areas where Lincoln's
Union Army was in control.

So . . . Harriet Tubman came to the
rescue!

Harriet Tubman

Tubman was already working for the Union Army. Now she was asked to sneak a regiment of former slaves into Confederate territory. The raid's purpose was to rescue slaves. And it was mighty dangerous!

The result? More than 700 slaves were rescued! And over 100 of them joined the Union Army.

Harriet Tubman was the *only* woman to lead a military operation during the Civil War.

African American soldiers in the Union Army

Slavery did not officially end until after the Civil War ended. On January 31, 1865, Congress passed the **13th Amendment to the U.S. Constitution**. It made slavery illegal.

At least 27 of the 36 states had to *ratify*—or approve—the 13th Amendment. This happened on **December 6, 1865**.

Slavery was finally ended everywhere in the United States.

But the freed slaves were not entirely free. ...

Sadly, many new laws were passed that limited the former slaves' freedom.

Passing the 13th Amendment in the House of Representatives

Above: A theatre for African Americans
Right: A "whites-only" taxi

The laws were called "Black Codes." They made it difficult for African Americans to be educated, to earn fair wages, or to move about freely.

Even in the North, African Americans were often *segregated*—or separated—from other people in public places.

It took America another *100 years* to outlaw unfair treatment of people based on the color of their skin. And this work is not finished!

When and Where Is Emancipation Celebrated?

The District of Columbia Emancipation Day

Emancipation Parade in Washington, D.C.

The District of Columbia Compensated Emancipation Act was signed on April 16, 1862. So April 16th was chosen as "D.C. Emancipation Day." It is celebrated only in D.C.

Emancipation Parades were held in Washington, D.C., from 1866 until 1901. After that, there were no parades for 100 years.

The parades were brought back in 2002. They are now grander than ever! Many events have been added to the celebration, from concerts to fireworks.

In 2004, April 16th became an official holiday in D.C.

The Emancipation Proclamation

"Juneteenth" in Texas

The State of Texas celebrates emancipation every year on June 19th—or "Juneteenth." Why?

Above: Reading the Emancipation Proclamation
Right: General Gordon Granger

On **June 19, 1865**, after the Civil War had ended, Union soldiers arrived in Galveston, Texas. General Gordon Granger read Lincoln's Emancipation Proclamation aloud.

More than 250,000 slaves were freed in Texas that day. They had not heard about the Emancipation Proclamation signed by President Lincoln two years earlier!

A Juneteenth parade in Houston, Texas

African Americans purchased land and built parks in Texas so they could celebrate Juneteenth.

Emancipation Park in Houston is the oldest of these parks. Former slaves collected $800 to buy the land in 1872. Recently, $34 million was spent on a spectacular make-over.

Booker T. Washington Park on the shores of Lake Mexia is another Juneteenth park. As many as 20,000 people gather here each year during the week-long celebration.

A child playing on a new basketball court in Emancipation Park, Houston

Juneteenth celebrations include music, speeches, ball games, and picnics with red food and drinks. But why *red*?

Red is a symbol of enslaved peoples' courage. So in Texas and elsewhere, Juneteenth picnics feature red food and drinks—like barbecue, red velvet cake, strawberry pie—and red soda pop!

Juneteenth celebrations serve a number of important purposes.

- Families can gather for annual reunions.
- Children can learn about slavery and the long struggle for emancipation.
- African Americans can celebrate their history, culture, and achievements.

A Juneteenth celebration in Florida

- All Americans can discuss ways to solve current problems caused by the long-lasting effects of slavery.
- Everyone can enjoy a day—or a week—of music, games, food, and fun!

Celebrating Juneteenth in Pennsylvania

In 1979, Juneteenth became an official state holiday in Texas. And Juneteenth celebrations have now spread to 45 other states.

The National Juneteenth Holiday Campaign is working to make Juneteenth a *national* holiday, celebrated in all 50 states.

Juneteenth would be like a 4th of July for African Americans!

Frederick Douglass would approve.